W9-BWF-477

Size

Many Ways to Measure

by Michele Koomen

Consultant:
Deborah S. Ermoian
Mathematics Faculty
Phoenix College
Phoenix, Arizona

Bridgestone Books
an imprint of Capstone Press
Mankato, Minnesota

Bridgestone Books are published by Capstone Press
151 Good Counsel Drive, P.O. Box 669, Mankato, Minnesota 56002
http://www.capstonepress.com

Library of Congress Cataloging-in-Publication Data
Koomen, Michele.
    Size: many ways to measure/by Michele Koomen.
    p. cm.—(Exploring math)
    Includes bibliographical references and index.
    ISBN 0-7368-3373-0 (paperback) ISBN 0-7368-0821-3 (hardcover)
    1. Mensuration—Juvenile literature. [1. Measurement. 2. Size.] I. Title. II. Series.
QA465 .K66 2001
530.8—dc21   00-010562

Summary: Simple text, photographs, and illustrations introduce concepts of size such as
    length, height, weight, and volume, including measuring with standard and
    nonstandard units.

Editorial Credits
Tom Adamson, editor; Lois Wallentine, product planning editor; Linda Clavel, designer;
    Katy Kudela, photo researcher

Photo Credits
Artville/Jeff Burke and Lorraine Triolo, 18 (all)
Capstone Press/CG Book Printers, cover, 12
Gregg Andersen, 6 (all), 22
Kent and Donna Dannen, 4
Kimberly Danger, 8, 10, 14, 16, 20

1 2 3 4 5 6 08 07 06 05 04 03

Table of Contents

What Is Size?

These two dogs are not the same size. The brown dog is smaller than the gray dog. The gray dog is larger than the brown dog. Size tells us how large or small something is.

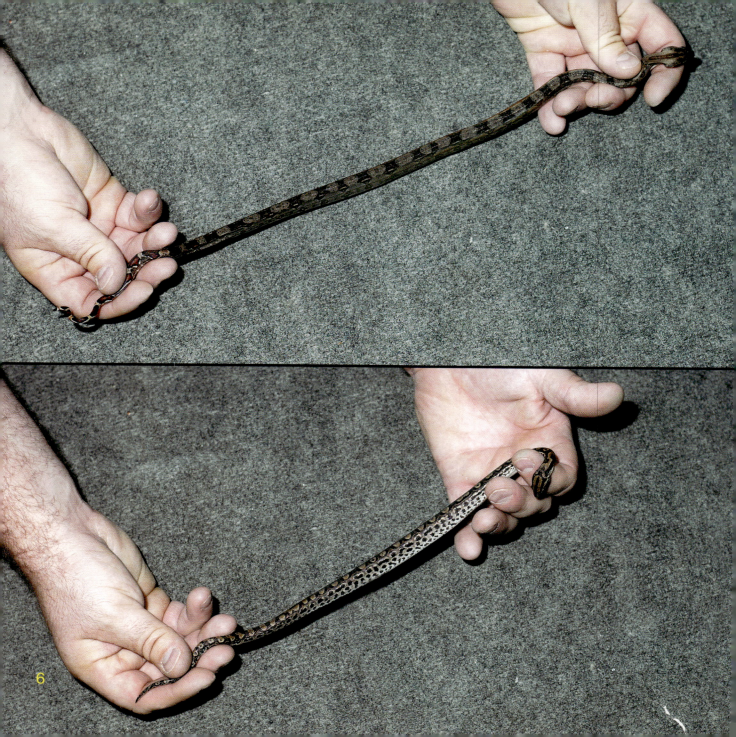

Length

These snakes are not the same length. The top snake is longer than the bottom snake. The bottom snake is shorter than the top snake. Length tells us how long or short something is.

Height

These kids are not the same height. We can compare the height of the kids when they stand next to each other. The girl is taller than the boy. The boy is shorter than the girl. Height tells us how tall or short something is.

Weight

Weight tells us how heavy or light something is. This bowling ball and this soccer ball are not the same weight. The bowling ball is heavier than the soccer ball. The soccer ball is easier to lift because it is lighter than the bowling ball.

Volume

Volume tells us how much a container can hold. This pitcher holds more juice than one glass does. Four glasses of juice fit in the pitcher.

Measuring with Pencils

We can measure the width of this table with pencils. This student placed pencils end to end across the table. The table is about 3 and one-half pencils wide.

Measuring with Crayons

A different student measured the same table with crayons. It is about 7 crayons wide. Why did they get different answers?

This bean is about 15 centimeters long.

This chili pepper is about 4 inches long.

Standard Units

Pencils and crayons are not the same length. That is why we use standard units to measure objects. Centimeters and inches are standard units for length. A ruler shows centimeters and inches.

Measuring with a Ruler

Each student measured the table again with a ruler. The table is 61 centimeters wide. Both students have the same answer this time. They also measured the table in inches. It is 24 inches wide.

Hands On: Measuring with Your Foot

What You Need

String
Marker
Scissors
An adult

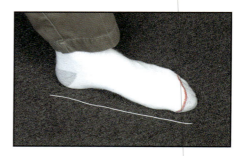

What You Do

1. Place the string on the floor. Place your foot on the string. Mark the string at your heel and at your big toe. Take your foot off the string. Cut the string at the two marks.
2. Use this piece of string to measure the length of a room, a desk, or the height of a door. Write down your measurement.
3. Measure an adult's foot to make another piece of string.
4. Measure the same objects with this piece of string. Why are the measurements different?

People use standard units of measurement, such as inches or centimeters. That way, everyone gets the same measurements. A foot is another standard unit of measurement. One foot equals 12 inches. How many inches long is your foot?

Words to Know

compare (kuhm-PAYR)—to point out how things are alike or different

height (HITE)—a measurement of how tall something is

length (LENGKTH)—the distance from one end of something to the other

measure (MEZH-ur)—to find how long, wide, or tall something is

standard (STAN-durd)—something that is widely used or accepted as correct; inches and centimeters are standard units of measurement; pencils and crayons are nonstandard units of measurement.

volume (VOL-yuhm)—the amount a container can hold

weight (WAYT)—the measure of how heavy a person or an object is

Read More

Adler, David A. *How Tall, How Short, How Faraway.* New York: Holiday House, 1999.

Bryant-Mole, Karen. *Size.* Mortimer's Math. Milwaukee: Gareth Stevens, 2000.

Cato, Sheila. *Measuring.* A Question of Math Book. Minneapolis: Carolrhoda Books, 1998.

Patilla, Peter. *Measuring.* Math Links. Des Plaines, Ill.: Heinemann Library, 2000.

Internet Sites

Ask Dr. Math
http://mathforum.com/dr.math
Figure This! Math Challenges for Families
http://www.figurethis.org
MathSteps
http://www.eduplace.com/math/mathsteps/index.html

Index